D0857539

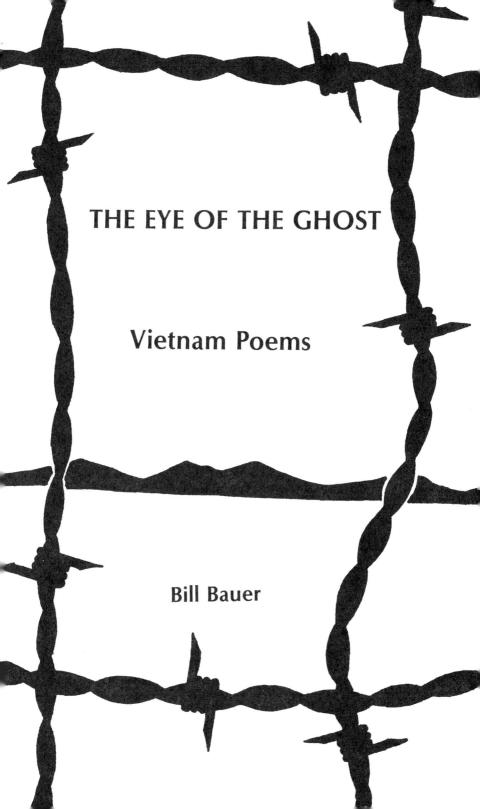

THE EYE OF THE GHOST

Vietnam Poems

Bill Bauer

Bruce Cutler, distinguished poet and director of the creative writing program at Wichita State University, selected **The Eye of the Ghost** from a group of sixty manuscripts submitted by Missouri writers for BkMk Press's Missouri Poet Contest. None of the manuscripts bore its author's name or publication credits. BkMk Press (UMKC) presented Bill Bauer with a $400 advance against royalties as well as publishing his first book.

Financial assistance for this project has been provided by the Missouri Arts Council, a state agency.

Library of Congress Cataloging-in Publication Data

Bauer, Bill, 1942-
  The Eye of the Ghost: Vietnam Poems

  1. Vietnamese Conflict, 1961-1975—Poetry.
I. Title.
PS3552.A8356E9 1986 811'.54 86-71527
ISBN O-933532-57-1 (pbk.)

.

Cover design by Wayne Pycior who served in Vietnam 1969-1970 in the 11th Armoured Cavalry Division

BkMk Press-UMKC

Dan Jaffe, Editor-in-Chief
Pat Huyett, Associate Editor
Pat Shields, Editorial Asst.

For Kathy,

Who lives my poems with me

CONTENTS

Vietnam Poems

Other Poems

Vietnam Poems

Capt. Thomas Falkenthal, a priest
from the Archdiocese of Chicago
serving with the Marine Battalion
Landing Team, said he worries when
he hears some troops say they want to
erase Lebanon from their memory.

"That kind of raises a caution flag,"
he said. "Because then it becomes a
ghost. Sometimes you have to look the
ghost in the eye."

— *The New York Times*
March 19, 1984

The Eye of the Ghost

The ghost shivers in one corner of the room
like an émigré from the moon.
You look over your shoulder
afraid it might speak.
If it speaks, you will remember.
To remember is to be a little crazy again.

The ghost remembers everything.
It has no stake in lying.
It remembers you were too afraid to say no.
You stood in line with the others and cursed your luck.
The line led to the bus, the bus to the plane,
the plane to the truck, the truck to the base-camp.
Rain dinged the tin rooves of hootches.
You really didn't know where you were, or why.

The ghost wanted you dead.
It was afraid, too,
digging tunnels one cupful at a time.
In the distance the floodlights of Tay Ninh
formed an enormous eye.
Bacon shriveled in the field stoves.
Ambush patrols crouched like lizards for a kill.
You spent the dry season eluding each other
and smoked when you could.

The ghost followed you home.
It was with you when you wrecked the car
and the neighbor's wife ran screaming into the yard.
An uncle told you:
"Let it go. Forget it. It's 5000 miles."
Fish in the aquarium swam oblivious to the crash
of mortars against the thin walls of daydreams.
You befriended the treefrogs and crickets again,

watched a thunderstorm blow by like twisted memory,
prayed it would carry the ghost away.

But a man meets his ghost in the hallway mirror,
brushes his teeth and locks the door.
He sleeps with a flashlight and a baseball bat.
The ghost squats in one corner of the room,
waiting for the dreamer to rise and stand its post.
In its eye as it watches
from its world on the other side of the sky,
You are the ghost.

Through a Helicopter Door

Turn back if you haven't the stomach.
It's not like the war on television.
Oil's smeared on the air.
Rotors kick you in the teeth
with dust and rock.
The next thing you know
you're on the ground
screaming for people.
You crawl and crawl,
but the only place to hide
is what you said goodbye to
when you became of age.

Al, War God

The man in the ball cap
at Oakland Airport
slapped them on the ass
as they ran,
late for a plane
and cheered "Go get'em, boys."
And they did.
And *they* did.

In Country

Fireballs blink
on Bien Hoa airstrip.
My bladder aches and I'm afraid,
but the Swedish girl says "Stay put;
the seat belt sign is on,"
and pokes out the overhead light.
I can smell her mix
of tension and perfume,
feel the splash of woman hair
against my face
one last time.

We circle, descend, circle,
then it's morning,
then it's real.
MP's rout us
off the Northwest Orient
into a furnace
of burning shit and JP4.
"Run, run," they shout,
"Run, run. You'll miss the bus.
You'll miss the bus to Long Bien."

Mama-sans,
heads wrapped in old cloth,
lean against wooden posts and yawn.
One drags a broom
in front of the banner,
WELCOME TO IV CORPS,
and turns to look,
but I look away.
I didn't know death
had such lively eyes.

Saturday Night
and Popcorn

I haven't been here long enough.
That's what's wrong with me.
I still look down
when USO girls bring popcorn
on their way to the officer's club.
I'm puzzled by the movie
lasered from the bunker
over two dozen young men
on blankets, cushions, lawn chairs,
making their beer ration last.

When the siren goes off
I scrounge with the others
for the nearest bunker,
huddled, with no weapon.
The sound track growls down.
The projector clicks to black.
It's a war again, and even then,
someone coughs.
I wait for the sappers
to toss canvas bags
into our middle:
Dead, age 22, of plastic explosive;
but two MP's with megaphones
tell us the alert is over.
Just a chopper
flipped on a power line,
pilot and gunner deep fried.

When I've been here long enough,
I'll stay with the others
to finish the movie and popcorn.
I won't go back to the hootch,
cry all night
and listen to a distant carbine
fill my dreams with lead.

An Act of Mercy

On my afternoon off
Mama-san cried
and held her jaw.
I drove her to the dental clinic
in the colonel's jeep
and read 52 pages
of Dostoevski.
Mama-san felt much better,
a gold tooth in her palm.
"Now I buy TV," she said.

Maidens

Water from a spigot
screwed to the belly
of a 250-pound bombshell
has the sound
of mama-sans chattering,
dunking fatigues in plastic pans.
Nothing I have said
will make them go,
and I don't care now.
I lost my privacy
at Ft. Carson Colorado.

I ignore their giggles,
try to get wet enough
to foam off
rice paddy sludge,
insect repellent,
chocolate bar,
dust on mud,
the captain saying,
"Last night's ambush was
a real success, men:
two dead,
three AK-47's,
five Chicom grenades,
knapsack with maps."
Bodies punctured
by claymore mines.

I was there,
I wasn't there,
I don't know.
The early morning heat,
splashing water,
women's voices,
say I wasn't there,
say I'm dreaming
on a sunporch
of a frame house
in a Missouri thunderstorm.

I haven't seen my body
in six days, maybe ten.
Ivory soap sliding
off my chest
says I wasn't there.

White body, brown face,
ghostself with dirt in my nails,
image on Time Magazine, CBS,
I bathe
in the laughter of maidens,
bombwater,
soap my hands,
my scalp,
my neck,
my legs,
my hips,
my gun almighty.
See, mama, all clean,
parts still connected.
Awaken me now and say
I'm already late for school.

Moonlight and a Breeze
(For Stephen Spender)

All that's left
is thunder now
and low-flying jets.
It's turning cool
and the land crabs are out.
He can smoke if he wants
and soften his grip on the stock,
but his peace will never come.
The boy who swang
on a Missouri porch
to summer wind
and an ice cream bell,
lost it, lost it all
the minute he spotted a figure
in his sights,
pulled the trigger
and meant it.

The Icehouse

I. Base Camp

From where I sat
in a five-ton truck
it seemed he'd always been there:
nineteen, no shirt,
prayer beads bangling
with ID tags,
grenade rings
around his bush hat.

They stood by the road
chanting: New guys, new guys,
greenhorn GI's.
Hey man, he said,
grabbing my gear,
move in with me.

Mostly we filled sandbags
or unloaded trucks
or after dark on bunker guard,
sandflies biting our faces,
told half true stories
of summer nights in Missouri.

We dreamed of a cool place,
And once on detail,
sat for five minutes
in the ice house,
a quonset hut
between the ammo dump and motor pool.
Blocks of murky ice
stood stacked in silver bars.
They kept the bodies there.
It was the only cool place.

Then there was an airlift
to Nui Ba Den.
You should have seen him
waiting for the Chinook,
joking around,

a stereo from Hong Kong in one hand,
a carbine in the other.
They ought to make a statue of it.

II. Mountain

The noises at night on Nui Ba Den
are ghosts of old Buddhists they said.
Cambodian tiger one thousand years old
hides in those caves they said.
In mists among large stones
he spliced a strobe light
into the generator,
watched it flicker
in our bunker.
Hey man, he said.
Let's make it like home;
make it like Kansas City.

We built partitions with
ammo boxes, bamboo screens,
hung posters of Colorado ski slopes,
rock and roll stars.
We swung in our hammocks
to the breezes of a GE fan.
We had it made up there.

Had it made until the rocket
shredded his clothes,
blew his billfold into a bush:
photographs, laundry receipts,
prescription for eye glasses,
shot record, best part of a letter,
five dollar bill.

III. Dream

We stacked him up
Naked and hard
In a dark icehouse,
His pubic hair
A blond willow tree,
His body
A silver kind of ice.

The Goldsmith's Daughter

*"This was once a country of artisans
and poets."—U.S. Army Colonel
watching detainees unload from a
truck at Cu Chi Base Camp*

Go, Buddha.
Go to the Cao Dai Temple.
Implore Jesus and Victor Hugo,
the All-Seeing Eye.
Tell them of the girl Ru,
squatting in the fishmarket.

I saw her there today,
hair hacked short,
mouth sunken and limp,
dust from the road
turning her gray in the sun.
Her family hides in the jungle.
She has sold her gold teeth,
her bracelets and chains.
They lead her through the basecamps
from one bunker to another,
her nose flowing muddy like the Mekong.
Now that her lover is beheaded
she gives them boom boom
for opium and five dollar bill.

Go, Buddha.
Tell them Ru was our hootch maid.
She brought us fresh flounder once.
She swept the floorboards clean.

The Company Clerk

Let's hear it for Alphonso,
going home at last,
goddamn him anyway.

Let's hear it for Alphonso.
He had a form for everything,
the inside track.

Need a mattress or a fan?
See Alphonso.
He'll get it for twenty-five.

Got a bronze star yet?
See Alphonso.
He'll write the commendation.

Want a dozen steaks or a Red Cross girl?
See Alphonso.
He'll arrange it.

One more time for little Alphonso.
He had all the right forms.
But one.

The Brotherhood of Man

There was me,
the Vietnamese,
and the rat.

The Vietnamese laughed
at the way I shaved,
at how I pulled my mouth
sideways and upwards
to tighten the skin.

He hung a single strand
14 inches long
from a mole on his cheek
that he stroked and admired
and held up to the lamp
so I could whistle at it.

But the warlord
of garbage and greed
mocked us both—
I shook when I saw him:
Two feet high on hind legs,
strutting the spotlight
by the latrine.
He bullied the night
through a stiff moustache
and a braggart's lip,
a sound that sobered me
where I stood:
Yeeeck! Yeeeck! Yeeeck!

Haircut

We heard two bursts
from an M-16:
One long, one short.

He must have stood
blocking the office door,
a Wolfhound
of the killer battalion
just in from the field,
the barrel of his weapon
in the other man's face:

I done like you said, First Sergeant,
the beard too, the moustache too.
Now look and tell me
I ain't no fightin' man.

The Chieu Hoi

Scrape a flounder
on a new piece of lumber.
Crack the egg on a stone
and drink it down.
War has such a sweet taste
when you're in the basecamp
and the sun is shining.
For now sleep boldly
in the middle of the day
and dream your life
the way it might have been.
Give the woman a name,
any name that suits you.
Don't worry about dying until tomorrow.
Make them sweat it out.

Viper

The rocket left its tube and
smoked through daybreak
over the wire,
so close to Position 28
I could feel its whistle
shoot static through my ear,
hear the nuts and bolts inside
shake down to the road
and a hoarse scream,
"Somebody help us over here, goddammit."

And so it arrived.
That night
it curled itself
around the wooden skid
where I slept,
dug in so deep
I closed my eyes to it.

In the village
from a distance it watched me
stiffen at the fingers of children
pulling at my pockets —
Were they children or devils?
I wondered, too,
those old women carrying baskets—
which one would strap a grenade
to the belly of a boy,
send him running at me
through the crowd?

It raced along the convoy
past ARVN soldiers
napping on the hulls of tanks
as we moved through the rubber
to Dau Tieng,
holding our M-50's two-handed,

ready for an ambush or sniper,
ready for another scream.

It breathed the rhythm
of my breath
as I lay awake
under the mosquito netting,
waiting for the rocket
with my name on it
to tear open the sandbagged roof.
I could feel B-52's shake the ground
all the way to Cambodia.
It suckered its sour lips
against my head and whispered:
Better them then you, eh GI?

Better them than you, eh GI?

War Dog

I shouldn't wonder why
you give me that streetwise snarl,
all teeth and head cocked,
ready to take me on.
I'm not prepared for another fight.
You can stand me off by yourself,
a lifer like you,
back against the bunker,
a head taller now than the other hounds.

Diaz called you puppy.
But you were never a puppy
and I was never a child.
You caught the rear wheel of a jeep
and I caught this war.

I've only come back to say goodbye,
to look around and say it happened.
This has to be quick,
I'm a short timer now,
Gear's turned in and orders cut.
They don't talk to me much.
I'm one of those who'll live.

It's not my fault
I got transferred.
It's not my fault
Diaz is dead.
Not much's sure in a place like this,
not even friends.
You do what you can.
The medics stitched your viscera
into its sac.
We stayed up all night,
an hour a man,
holding your leg
so the cast would set.

I can't squeeze back
what's been torn away.
But Butterball, my little puppy,
I leave you one thing sure.
The night I rocked and you cried
We held a moment of childhood.

Benediction

Men, the chaplain said,
my mission here today
is to pray with you
on your departure
from the combat area
and thank the lord almighty
You survived this tour
without death or maiming injury.
But before I get into that,
I want to remind you
there's a war going on
and it's not going to stop
because you got orders.
Even now the North Vietnamese
move into the Angel's Wing.
Your buddies are being airlifted
into a jungle
of booby traps, mines, malaria, ambush,
and you can help.
Sergeant Zigmunt has the forms.
Re-up and get a bonus.
Don't forget the early out
or assignment of your choice.
Now let us pray
in the name of the Joint Chiefs of Staff
and fixed-wing aircraft
and the napalm's orange glare
So help you god.

Private Armistice

Philip, my little brother:
In the photograph
of my homecoming
I see hands hold you high
over friends and uncles
and you don't know me:
One hundred twenty-seven pounds
in dress green,
the sides of my head
still shaved white,
my new smile
a covert operation.

War Stories

Old men of the VFW—
put down your mugs
and listen up.
I have a story, too.
It's about the face
of a second lieutenant
I keep seeing in my dreams.
He staggers bareheaded
onto the road,
the road out there
in the rubber plantation.
He's holding up
a No. 10 envelope
with the remains of one of your sons
bone slivers
scraped with a bayonet
from the hull of the APC
he sent down Highway One.

He just keeps coming at me,
holding out someone's soul
for the U.S. Mail,
his face a map
of all the roads we marched down,
one boot after the other
into all the trophy cases
of your goddamned VFW halls.

You tell me how it ends.
You got all the answers.

Rabbit Hunting

I

Slugs from a twenty-two pump
shattered the snow.
The rabbit zigzagged grass clumps
frozen stiff above the surface,
tumbled high in the air,
recovered, bounded into the woods.
They chased it five minutes or more
before losing it in the twisted
scrub oak, gullies and piss elm.
Uncle Joe was there, Little Joe, Robert and him.

The woods held the cold close to the ground,
numbing his feet in his boots.
He had not fired the shotgun that day;
They cursed a wasted shot.
He kept thinking of beef stew and hot chocolate,
heat by the stove in the farmhouse.

Then he saw it bobbing in the brush,
circling away from their voices.
It clawed forward, dragging its rump,
leaving the snow red.
He waited until it reached the ditch
not five feet away,
watched it paw down the slope,
flattened its head with a direct blast.

II

Home two weeks
he buttoned borrowed corduroy,
walked in a line
with his cousins and uncles
as they always had,
heading north from the tractor shed.

Not twenty yards out
a rabbit behind a combine wheel,
a small gray rabbit,
panicked, paddled a drift
for a place in the trash pile.

He squatted, sighted, military style,
elbows on his knees, ready to fire,
but stood up and spat a blood oath:
I will not shoot another living thing.
By god, I will not.

Taps

My Uncle Roy
drives a truck
that spreads salt
during snowstorms.
He doesn't want to hear
my yakety-yak
about Cambodia and all that.
The world's already got
too much shitass misery.

Sideglance

I am the bastard boy
of the World Wars,
born into a violent time
in a violent country.
Violence is what I know.
Violent is what I am.
But don't worry, mister,
I won't kill you.
My dreams more than satisfy this urge
to lick the bones of the dead.

Joy

The soldier who kills for fun can laugh at anything, but the man who was robbed of his laughter by the killing searches for it everywhere. Sometimes he encounters the shipping crate in his basement and says, "I should have thrown this away long ago," and pries open the lid. He sorts through the socks, underwear, camouflaged boots, medallions, propaganda leaflets and a pearl-handled bowie knife inscribed with his name and "4th of the 9th Infantry, Manchu." "I should have thrown this away long ago," he says again, trying to feel how it was, the day after First Grade, slamming the metal wheels of his skates into the sidewalk, the wind lifting him up by the hair, and laughing, laughing, laughing. But his voice only circles the barrel of his throat, his laughter mute as army green, coarse as a kettledrum.

Last Poem

Today I wrote my last Vietnam poem,
Fifteen years after the fact.
Those folk songs, those anti-war chants—
I couldn't get rid of them.
I'd hear someone screaming,
shattered or shot;
I'd plan my revenge
for gung-ho colonels and academic fools.

But alone in a house
in the middle of February,
I only see a familiar room.
I can look out a window
into a brown and leafless wood
and know there's an end
to anger and sorrow.
I guess you just retire it.

Other Poems

Out There

In my Great Flying Dream
I can skim a whole sky
with one flick of a foot.

My loop de loops
trace memory
above rush hour traffic,
white, wingless motion
willed only by desire.

Myrna, the middle-aged goddess,
waves from a street corner
with a used hanky,
waves off all gravity
as a serious mistake.
"Come back, *mon amour*," she wails.
"Don't get lost, out there, *mon chéri*."

I want so much to please her
my backward ovals
spin me out of understanding,
out over the scrub oak of Oklahoma,
across Texas and into the Gulf,
out into all those possibilities
I've been told
Just might be a possibility.

Spring Clover

My mother's a stranger to me
in the country,
and I am a stranger
in my mother's country.
A city kid in penny loafers,
I stumble through meadow grass,
dodge the buzz of dragonfly
off cattail.

All year long
she doesn't say much,
but on a Missouri highway,
past framed fields
and sagging fruit stands,
she points and calls them out,
"Soybeans! Alfalfa!
Kaffircorn! Spring clover!"

She catalogues
Uncle Harry's place
with a twisted stick:
storm cellar, feedbin,
boysenberry patch, poison oak,
hedgeapple grove.
In the land of fodder
and new milk
she still climbs fences.

Marie, she's called down here,
slicing ham in a farmhouse kitchen
full of aunts and uncles
so pruned in the face
you can't tell man from woman;
Marie, who lives in town now,
knows when to plant,
when to pick,
how to stomp rabbits from brushpiles,

why store eggs have gone pale.

After dishes
she walks alone
in a barnyard of banty hens
and tractor ruts
past a shattered hog chute
she once named Corn Cob Trail,
pokes a turkey feather into a cob,
tosses it high,
watches it spin, spin down.

Heading back,
we stop by Uncle Ray's.
I see her there in her country,
the girl, again the girl,
hair black as shade,
leaning over
a natural spring well:
When the ladle dips,
tiny fish scatter
in the pupils of her eyes.

A Fear of the Ball

He snapped his head
just before
the ball hit the plate,
a fuzzy mass
that might have sprung
from centerfield
or at the edge of vision,
sucking him
into a sequence of angles
turned in on themselves.

No matter
what he told himself
or the steps of thought
he measured to that point,
it happened.
His head shot up and held
like a deer
cast in headlights.

He could feel his eyes
wrap it all inside.
He could hear the smack smack
of the second baseman's glove,
the infield bleating,
"Hey babe hey babe hey babe."

Shoveling Snow, 1952

My Austrian grandmother
stands by a window
listening to my shovel scrape
the snow as it falls.

By tomorrow
my jagged path
will disappear again
into smoothness,
but she worries
that school children,
small and wrapped in wool,
may lose their way
if sidewalk slides into snowdrift.

Tonight when this work is done
I will sit in stocking feet
at a table steaming
with liver dumplings and broth,
sip homebrew
until I feel numb and good.

Grandfather will smoke Luckies
by an old Philco,
half hearing Vaughn Monroe
sing "Shine on
Shine on harvest moon
Up in the sky...."

She will turn up the oven
to give me warmth,
lean towards me on an elbow
and tell again
how poor they were in the old country.

All About Trees

Woman, says the Good Book,
was crafted of man's bone.

That's a lie.

She spread open her loam,
and he sprang up.
The wind showed them
how to survive the seasons.

Tough Love

What that boy lacked was
a heavy dose of old-fashioned ways,
a limitation on his mouth and mind,
the strap of the covenant and Biblical bread.
Nature left without a course
grows wild and out of bounds,
seeks perverse corners,
needs direction for its crazy moves,
the preacher said.

They gave him this gift of love,
a love so tough
it locked him in his room
and he spread it across the wall
with his daddy's two-ten.
"Guess I just ain't much good,"
his note read.

A Craving Like Onyx

My mouth can't have
what it wants when it wants it,
an afternoon that yields
the taste of its longing,
a suck for its suck,
the right word clearly spoken.

At night its tongue
probes the hammered walls
with a soft claw
for the missing ingredient.

Far down the gorge
the mad handler
both beats it forward
and reins it back.
It thrashes and digs
for a surface
that, when it comes,
leaves it lapping at air
and forms like glass
over the swallowed demand:
"Give it to me;
Give it to me now."

All Fathers Must Die
(Three Nightmares)

I. Falling

The blow
uproots me,
a sapling
torn by wind,
ejects me
off the world,
freefalling
to a black hole
at the bottom of space.

Shock waves
reverberate
into the stratosphere.
Continents, oceans blaze.
Beggars riot in New Delhi.

Perched above the dream
on a smoking fragment,
I pack cartridges,
watch my shape
sinking:

The pale infant head,
spinning target eyes,
mouth of sparrow beak
tumbling,
clawing
anti-matter.

II. Eyes

I am followed
by hooded men
stretching rubber legs
from tree to tree
along night streets
in the old neighborhood,

hissing.

Spotlights from their eyes
crisscross the pavement,
but I pretend not to notice.
If I just stay calm and don't run
they might call it off—
dogs bored with their own snarling.

I keep telling myself
"Turn down an alley,
crawl through a window,
wait as they slide by."
In the streetlight
I see the barbed wire barricade.

What offense has been committed?
Why do they follow
but never attack?
"Who are you?" I shout,
"What do you want?
Give me more than echoes."

Their light tubes converge.
I can't run,
legs too heavy and
it's strapped to my back
like a guitar.

I prepare for an assault
that never comes,
just one large eye
opening above the sycamores.

I climb its beam,
poke my head into a socket,
squeeze, wriggle through,
tumble
into a field of flowers.

I hear myself laughing,
"Aha....so this is how it is,"
and float like cottonseed
on a warm wind,

inhaling
chrysanthemum,
dahlia,

orchid.

III. Machine Gun Fire

The car has no driver.
It takes the curves
at ninety-six.
Crouched in the back seat,
hands chained to ankles,
I wait for the crash.

The car fishtails
through stoplights,
railroad crossings,
striped road blocks,
plunges over
the hill's crest
banging parked cars,
light poles, curbings,
the retaining walls,
that funnel it
into plate glass.

They stand near the pool table
under mobster hats,
chalking cue sticks,
laughing at the wreckage,
at me broken on the floor.
They are all here—
Unmasked
fathers, grandfathers,
generations of anger,
clucking tongues,
wagging fingers,
pursing lips.

I find the leather case,
unpack each carefully oiled part,
assemble it,

adjust the sling,
load, release the bolt—
chink, chunk—
tuck it under my arm,
and then I fire
scattering brain bit and bone.

Before this is over
I will kill them all,

All.

Horses Dancing in the Snow

A stray cloud from the Rockies
brought snow and a high-up scent,
flakes the size of half dollars
sudden through the April morning.
Horses in a field
downhill from the road
scattered at the sound
of snow out of season,
struck at it with their hooves,
crisscrossed the meadow grass,
their tails waving a rhythm
to outstretched legs.
They whinnied and bucked
along the barbed wire fence
and quick as the snow stopped,
reared and circled back,
put their noses together,
shook winter off.

Francis Wilhelm Bauer
1874-1959

Lost in a fever
he struggled blankets off,
tore at tubes
in his nose and arm,
mumbled something in German
over black nubs of teeth.
"Grandpa," I said. "Lie still."

But he wrestled me back,
and the nurses came,
five of us pushing a man
down on his deathbed,
because we knew what was best.

The raspy sound of his voice
still hurts.
Out of breath,
his hair wet against the pillowcase,
the Bull of Steinberg pleaded to me
from deep in his gut,
"Grandson! Make them go away!"

In the Reign of Our Terror

"There was a steel pole running
from the floor to the ceiling
behind Gray's chair, and we watched
him slam his head into the pole for
eight minutes as hard as he could."
—Newsweek, April 9, 1984

Some execute their wayward
with a square-shaped gun
held perpendicular to the skull,
and the forehead lights up
as if, by god,
interjected with a new idea.

So dirty dogma deals
by sleight of hand,
by valve, by syringe, by kilowatt,
to lull, burn, shake
the cripple from his insight.

We don't proclaim our madness
on a street corner by the Ritz,
but we tie our shoes
and button each button,
and our insanity gurgles
in the throat of a man
strapped by intravenous tubes—
the rapist and killer
who acts out your anger and mine.

Suburban hangman,
What does the gray matter?
When not to fold, bend or mutilate
matters more than
the clatter of the guillotine,
the bang of a trap door,
the steam of your witness
hyperventilating against the glass.

A Brief Analysis
of The Situation

People who don't speak
in their natural voices
look to see if you are watching them
formulate their next policy statement.

The manipulation of the facial tissue
in conjunction with an elevation in the throat
produces a most important sound
and a reapportionment of the lower lip.

She might be an anchor woman
describing riots in another world.
He's testifying before a sub-committee
in expert cadence and pitch.

Listen to me, they keep saying,
I'm alone in a hotel room
eleven stories above it all.
I'm out of cigarettes and falling asleep
with the New York Times
smeared all over my hands.

Going to See Where She Was Born

Something about a long blue Oldsmobile
with Kansas City plates
makes a man in a red CO-OP hat
drive his tractor down the middle of the road.
"Go slow," she tells me. "In Peabody, Kinsley and Offerle,
they still have hanging judges."

Tumbleweeds chase us like dustblown posses
all the way to Dodge City
where the lock up for licker is nine.
We roll softly through the center of town,
headed for the Silver Spur Lodge,
1510 Wyatt Earp Blvd.
Inside our room a notice taped to the door
tells all us nice folks:
"YOUR DAY ENDS AT 12 O'CLOCK NOON."
"Tomorrow," she says, "we'll go meet mother."

Next thing, we hear semi's thumping by.
The travel alarm reads 12:36 PM.
We sit on the edge of the bed,
naked and soaked with love,
waiting for the sheriff to come.

Calling Time

Face it, there's more than
a jump shot and high caliber pass,
but not much.
It's the basket at the buzzer you remember.
A few mistakes are all you get.

These late August mornings I wake the neighbors
with the wham wham of a basketball.
He who cursed their self-propelled's
rises early now, sleepless again,
scanning the scoreboard
for judgment day in bankruptcy court.
They pretend not to know
but stop waving from backporches.
The birds broadcast the verdict
from yard to yard: Fouled out! Fouled out!

This house I painted three times by hand
and stopped all the leaks.
My trees took fifteen years to look their age.
We raised the hoop on a birthday bash,
four of us or more, enough for two on two,
slurring our words and missing the rim.
But one season tumbles into another.
McArty, local twenty-one champ,
doesn't have time anymore,
running, running for school board.
Ace Rivera, all-state guard,
would rather just drink.
My son, I pushed off with advice.
My daughter, gone too, I ignored.
From a bedroom window someone still watches me
execute a textbook lay up
and drive across the centerline into middle age.

Yet here in the fast break of autumn
I can maneuver from mid-court to the key,

opposed by no one but myself:
Back off, switch hands,
pivot into the choreography
of hook shot, sky and rebound.
Each quarter ends by my own clock.
In this world of dribblers and shooters
the closest distance between two points
is over the top.

One day when I have gone to buy the bread
they will come to post a final score
on the bat and board of my small, unthrifty life.
I will surrender none of my private strategies,
but they can carry off
high blood pressure, tics, gastric distress.
In the confusion of their full court press
I will signal a calling of time,
stop competing, be myself again.
Even the grubs gnawing the bluegrass will know
I'll play again in another kind of season.

Notes On
THE EYE OF THE GHOST

An Act of Mercy
For many Vietnamese gold teeth and jewelry served as a savings account.

Maidens
Bombshells were often used as water tanks. A pipe and faucet were screwed into the belly of the bombshell to make a field shower.

The Goldsmith's Daughter
The Cao Dai is a religious sect with a following of two million Vietnamese. Their temple in Tay Ninh is filled with gold objects and is famous for a single large eye behind the sanctuary. The Cao Dai's patron saints are Buddha, Victor Hugo and Jesus.

The Chieu Hoi
Chieu Hoi means "open arms." The Army instituted the Chieu Hoi program to induce the Viet Cong to surrender. They were given amnesty in exchange for information or duty as scouts. Many had been fighting in the jungle, living in tunnels and caves, since they were small children. Many of them, too, were executed during the American withdrawal by their own people.

Benediction
The Angel's Wing is a section of Vietnam near the Cambodian border, so called because of its shape on a military map.

Bill Bauer published his first poem at age eight when he read aloud a tribute entitled, "My Aunt Ann." Since then he has hidden most of his poems. He has worked as a caddy, shoeshine boy, truck driver for a bottling company, home improvement salesman, bill collector, laborer in a plastics factory, psychiatric aide, newspaper reporter for *The Kansas City Star*, and an underwriter of specialty insurance coverages. He once catalogued all of the philosophers whose works are shelved at the Rockhurst College Library. He is president of Media/Professional Insurance, Inc. in Kansas City, Missouri. A graduate of Rockhurst College, Bauer attended the graduate program at UMKC and the Longboat Key Writers Conference, where he worked with John Ciardi. He is married and the father of two children.

Bauer's National Guard Unit was activated during the riots of 1968 and he was sent to Vietnam the following year.

Other Books from BkMk Press

Missouri Short Fiction, edited by Conger Beasley, Jr. 23 short stories by Missouri writers including Bob Shacochis, Speer Morgan, James McKinley, John Mort, Charles Hammer, David Ray and others. $8.95

Voices from the Interior, edited by Robert Stewart. Poems by over 50 of Missouri's finest poets. $6.50

Modern Interiors, by Stephen Gosnell. Quality lithographic reproductions with short interrelated fictional pieces. $12.95

Selected Poems of Mbembe Milton Smith. "One of our most nourishing poets... He used language deftly with lively, affectionate respect." — Gwendolyn Brooks. $8.95

Artificial Horizon, by Laurence Gonzales. "...a first rate young writer whose work merits attention from anyone seeking lively idiom, authentic detail and a fresh point of view..." — Edward Abbey. $8.95

In the Middle: Midwestern Women Poets, edited by Sylvia Wheeler. Poems & essays by Lisel Mueller, Faye Kicknosway, Joan Yeagley, Diane Hueter, Sonia Gernes, Janet Beeler Shaw, Roberta Hill Whiteman, Dorothy Selz & Cary Waterman. $9.50

Dark Fire by Bruce Cutler. A book-length narrative poem, "...a lively, imaginative, and finely crafted tale of modern life." — Judson Jerome in *Writer's Digest.* $6.25

Wild Bouquet, by Harry Martinson, The first American collection of these nature poems by the Swedish Nobel Laureate. Translated and with an introduction by William Jay Smith and Leif Sjöberg. $10.95 cloth

Writing in Winter by Constance Scheerer. "...one of the fresher voices out of the Midwest...vivid and memorable." — David Ray $5.25

Hi-Fi & The False Bottom by Goran Stefanovski. Two plays by a well-known Yugoslavian playwright, translated from the orginal Macedonian. Introduction by James McKinley. $8.50

Tanks, short fiction by John Mort. "The most vivid and upsetting piece of writing on Vietnam that I've ever read." — Peter Meinke. $8.95

BkMk PRESS-UMKC
College of Arts & Sciences

University of Missouri-Kansas City
5216 Rockhill Rd., Rm. 204
Kansas City, MO 64110-2499